Tao Quotes

Tao Quotes

The Ancient Wisdom of the Tao Te Ching by Lao Tzu

Stefan Stenudd

Stefan Stenudd is a Swedish author, artist, and historian of ideas. He has published a number of books in Swedish as well as English, both fiction and non-fiction. Among the latter are books about Taoism, the cosmology of the Greek philosophers, the Japanese martial arts, life force concepts, Tarot imagery and astrology.

In the history of ideas he studies the thought patterns of creation myths, but also Aristotle's Poetics. He is an aikido instructor, 6 dan Aikikai Shihan, former Vice Chairman of the International Aikido Federation, member of the Swedish Aikido Grading Committee and President of the Swedish Budo & Martial Arts Federation. He has his own extensive website:
www.stenudd.com

Also by Stefan Stenudd:
Tao Te Ching: The Taoism of Lao Tzu Explained, 2011.
Cosmos of the Ancients: The Greek Philosophers on Myth and Cosmology, 2007.
Life Energy Encyclopedia, 2009.
Qi: Increase Your Life Energy, 2008.
Aikido Principles, 2008.
Attacks in Aikido, 2008.
Aikibatto: Sword Exercises for Aikido Students, 2007.
Tarot Unfolded, 2012
Your Health in Your Horoscope, 2009.
All's End, 2007.
Murder, 2006.

Stefan Stenudd's Taoism Website:
www.taoistic.com

Tao Quotes: The Ancient Wisdom of the Tao Te Ching by Lao Tzu.
Copyright © Stefan Stenudd, 2013
Book design and calligraphy by the Stefan Stenudd.
All rights reserved.
ISBN: 978-91-7894-060-8
Publisher: Arriba, Malmö, Sweden, info@arriba.se
www.arriba.se

Contents

道

Preface

Taoism is not a religion. It's all about here and now: how to live a pleasant life, without causing unnecessary commotion or distress. Tao, the Way, is a law of nature behind all of creation. Those who can harmonize with it will be at peace with existence.

The oldest and major source to Taoism is *Tao Te Ching* (also spelled *Dao De Jing*), which translates to *The Book on the Way and Virtue*. It was written by the legendary Lao Tzu (Lao Zi) sometime during the 6th and the 4th century BC in China. The old classic still has a lot to teach us.

Tao Te Ching consists of 81 chapters about the Way: its mystery, its cosmology, and what it teaches us about how to conduct our lives the wisest.

In this book, 389 quotes from the 81 chapters are sorted according to their themes. That is not the case in the Tao Te Ching, where the chapters appear in an order that seems at least partly due to chance - or maybe the writer's impulse, while composing the book. It's also possible that the book is a collection of proverbs from different sources, done long ago by someone else than their original author or authors.

I hope that by sorting quotes from the chapters into themes, it will be easier for the reader to examine Lao Tzu's thoughts on different subjects. The Tao Te Ching chapters often return to certain topics, making similar or just slightly altered statements about them. When the Tao quotes are sorted according to themes, it's possible to see the patterns of Lao Tzu's thoughts more clearly and to explore them at depth.

The translation of the Tao Te Ching chapters in this book is my own, mainly based on these Chinese versions: Wang Pi (Wang Bi in pinyin), the two manuscripts of Mawangdui, and that of Guodian. A great number of translations into Western languages, mostly but not only English, have also been consulted.

For a fully commented translation of the Tao Te Ching with the chapters in their established order, please see my book *Tao Te Ching. The Taoism of Lao Tzu Explained*.

Introduction

Taoism is a Chinese philosophy dating back to at least the 4th century BC, probably a hundred or so years before that. Some call it a religion, which is questionable since it contains almost nothing about divinities or the afterlife. Instead, it's a gentle philosophy of life, teaching how to live in accordance with nature and find balance within oneself as well as in society.

The oldest and major source to Taoism is the book *Tao Te Ching*, consisting of 81 short chapters that should more rightly be called verses, presenting the cosmology and philosophy of Taoism.

Lao Tzu

The legendary writer of the Tao Te Ching is Lao Tzu. He is supposed to have lived in the 6th Century BC. The birth year 604 BC is mentioned here and there in texts about him, but the certainty of it is doubtful. Experts disagree on whether he ever existed. The Tao Te Ching might be a compilation of separate texts and sayings, without one single author. But then again, it could also be that one man's work.

The name Lao Tzu is honorific. It means Old Master and has also been used as a title for the Tao Te Ching text. It is still in such use among many scholars.

Legend has it that he was an older contemporary of K'ung Tzu, Confucius, who lived 551 to 479 BC and whose existence is well documented in historical sources. The life of Lao Tzu, on the other hand, was not explicitly recorded until *Shih chi*, the book of Chinese history written by Ssu-ma Ch'ien around 90 BC.

Lao Tzu, Old Master. Calligraphy by Stefan Stenudd.

道 Tao

He even describes a meeting between Lao Tzu and K'ung Tzu in 517 BC, when K'ung visited the capital of Chou. The former is portrayed as both older and wiser.

Age equaled wisdom and superiority in ancient China, and Confucianism was the leading philosophy already soon after the death of its creator, so Taoists would have wished for Lao Tzu to be the senior of the two. Thereby, his thoughts would gain the prestige of being of older origin.

The legend about him says that he worked as a highly respected civil servant at the court of Chou, where he managed the royal archives. At old age, he had grown tired of all the deceit, politics, and hypocrisy of the court, so he left the country riding on a water buffalo. This is the most common depiction of him, heading for the border on a water buffalo.

At the northwestern border, he stayed the night in the house of a warden of the barrier gate, Yin Hsi, who was so impressed by his wisdom that he urged Lao Tzu to write it down before leaving. So he did.

Then he crossed the border, and nothing more is known about his fate.

Tao Te Ching

The primary source to Taoism is the book *Tao Te Ching*, one of the ancient Chinese classics. The three words of the title are *Tao*, way, *Te*, virtue, and *Ching*, classic: The Classic of the Way and Virtue. The word Ching refers to a book that has become a classic, a scripture revered as sacred, transmitting wisdom of old, deemed fundamental to Chinese culture and philosophy.

The most ancient manuscript of the Tao Te Ching found so far is that from Guodian (Kuo-tien), dated to around 300 BC. It is far from complete, but its existence proves that the text appeared no later than in the 4th century BC.

The oldest almost complete versions of the book are the two manuscripts found in Mawangdui (Ma-Wang-tui), from around the year 200 BC, one a few years older than the other. All other manuscripts are significantly younger.

Spelling

The transcription of Chinese, how to write its words with Western letters, is not an exact science. Since Chinese texts are written with pictograms, little is stated about the actual pronunciation. That differs considerably through China, both geographically and historically. Without specifications of the sounds in their written language, this diversity was unavoidable.

There are two major methods of transcription at use today for Chinese words. Pinyin is the one presented by the modern state of China in the 1950's as the official system of transcription. Today, it's the system used almost exclusively, especially for anything contemporary.

In the case of the Chinese classics, though, an older system of transcription is well established and still in use. It's called Wade-Giles after its two creators, the latter of which published a Chinese-English dictionary based on it, in 1892. This system of transcription was the dominating one in the English language for most of the 20th century, so all the translated classics of that period used it. Therefore, it's the spelling we are still the most familiar with, especially in the case of the Chinese classics and their terminology.

In this book, I stick to Wade-Giles for all the words in Lao Tzu's text, as well as for names and terms related to it. That way, it's much easier for the reader to compare this version to most of the previous ones in English.

Here are some examples of words and names, as they are transcribed according to Wade-Giles and pinyin:

Wade-Giles	Pinyin
Tao Te Ching	Dào Dé Jing (or Daodejing)
Lao Tzu	Lao Zi (or Laozi)
K'ung Tzu	Kong zi (or Kongzi)
Chuang Tzu	Zhuang Zi (or Zhuangzi)
I Ching	Yì Jing (or Yijing)
Ch'i	qì (or qi)
Yin yang	yin yáng (or yin yang)
T'ai chi	tàijí (or taiji)
Sheng jen	shèng rén
Wu-wei	wúwéi
Wang Pi	Wang Bi
Shih chi	Shijì
Ssu-ma Ch'ien	Sima Qian
Ma-wang-tui	Mawángdui (or Mawangdui)
Kuo-tien	Guodiàn (or Guodian)

Tao Themes

In spite of its mere 5,000 words, the content of the Tao Te Ching is not easy to penetrate and grasp. Its minimized language and poetic form of expression open for a wide variety of interpretations. That has been evident in commentaries through the centuries, sometimes revealing pure bewilderment. Present day interpretations have not changed that.

Still, even a first reading reveals a basic pattern. The Tao Te Ching clearly focuses on a limited number of major themes or topics:

The Way
Virtue
The Sage
Non-action
Moderation
Ruling
War

Of course, some other subjects are also treated, but the whole text is mainly occupied by the above seven themes, touching any other subject briefly and within the above mentioned contexts. Those themes cover the content of the Tao Te Ching well, but what can be discussed is what chapter belongs to which theme. They often overlap.

Still, the division into themes is necessary in the process of understanding what Lao Tzu has to say about the subjects he contemplates. The 81 chapters hop between them, treating them from different angles or repeating with almost the same wording what has already been stated. This becomes clear and accessible when reviewing the chapters accordingly.

道

The seven themes are no surprise, considering the nature of Lao Tzu's philosophy.

The Way

Tao, the Way, is the core and essence of Taoism, and the major theme of the Tao Te Ching. It can be described as the idea of a primordial law of nature by which the universe has been given its shape and mechanics. Tao is the way the world works. This law made the world spring into being and keeps on ruling how all things in the world behave.

Lao Tzu was not the first to use the term with such a splendid meaning. Since ancient times, Chinese tradition talked about *Tien Tao*, the Way of Heaven, referring to much the same – how nature was ruled. But Lao Tzu had much to say about the characteristics of this way of nature, and in what direction it leads the world as well as everything and everyone in it. That's what occupies a substantial number of the chapters.

Lao Tzu hints at a primordial chaotic state, before the world emerged. Tao must have been present there, as well, or chaos would have remained forever. Whether Tao was born somehow in that chaos or just rested before springing into action at some point, Lao Tzu is unable to decide.

He hesitates before the paradox of getting something out of nothing, as have so many philosophers since. But he does state clearly that the world had a beginning, although it must remain an impenetrable mystery exactly out of what the world emerged. When it did, though, it was the work of Tao.

Tao created the world by bringing order to the chaos, simply by commanding it to conform to its law. From a state so disorderly that nothing could be made or perceived of it, Tao built the universe as a matter of giving it structure, taming it into a system bound by its primary natural law.

In that sense, it's indeed comparable to a law of nature in modern physics like, say, gravity. It decides how the universe behaves, ever since its emergence at the Big Bang. But Tao is described as the one law ruling all others. Therefore, the best comparison would be with the idea of a united field theory, a basic law of nature behind every phenomenon in the universe.

Yet, Lao Tzu's Tao is more than an impersonal natural force acting like a fixed mathematical formula. It contains meaning and purpose. It has intention and a direction, though not at all like the deity of a religion, dictating its will and relating more or less emotionally to creation. Still, Tao has an aim and clear preferences.

Well, Lao Tzu is not crystal clear about this. His words can also be interpreted as suggesting the will of the Tao law of nature just being a way of looking at it: Since Tao is how nature really works, it can be described as a willful intention of this law of nature. It's how it is, whether it's meaningful or not. Lao Tzu certainly finds it to be for the best, but he also concludes that it would be pointless and gruesome to resist it.

What can be ascertained about Lao Tzu's Tao is that resistance against it is futile, whereas accepting it makes everything smoother. That's simply because the Tao law of nature rules everything. Again, this comes strikingly close to our understanding of the laws of nature.

In several of the chapters about Tao, Lao Tzu marvels at the seeming paradox of the world being ruled by some hidden law of nature, which regulates everything without pal-

道

pable means. The manifest world is run by an invisible force, a principle, which is itself untouchable, unshakable, inexhaustible.

Gravity is a good illustration to Lao Tzu's impression of the Tao law of nature. It's an invisible force commanding everything, endlessly and seemingly without any effort. A man may struggle to lift a big stone from the ground, but as soon as he lets go it falls back to the ground, bringing that effort to naught. We have learned why, at least we have it somewhat figured out, but to the ancient mind this was a mystery worth pondering.

Lao Tzu enjoys the example of water, which ceaselessly moves towards the lowest point, as if exceedingly humble by nature. When the water pours downhill, it seems to be a force contained within the water itself. We know that it's gravity pulling it downwards. Lao Tzu may not have understood that, but his ideas about Tao suggest that he surmised it. Water follows Tao, which commands things to lower themselves, as if humility is the aim and the ideal of this law of nature.

In that way, Tao is a law of nature acting like an ideal – as if the power of that law is the ideal.

This is not that far from Plato's theory of ideas, regarding ideal forms as the true molds of the universe as we see it. Both Plato and Lao Tzu contemplate the same mystery: What makes things get their fixed shapes and behave according to their fixed patterns?

The difference is that where Plato suggests multiple laws or conditions, Lao Tzu presumes that there is but one law, Tao, behind every condition. And this law rules the universe by the irresistible power of yielding.

So, Lao Tzu teaches that we should understand Tao in

order to adjust our lives accordingly. We should learn to yield to the ultimate power of yielding.

Virtue

Te, Virtue, is one of the most important concepts in Tao Te Ching. That's why the word is also in the title. It can be explained as the noble behavior of a person who follows Tao, the Way, which is virtuous in itself. We imperfect human beings, though, have to learn it.

So, Te has no value of its own. It's not an active force in the world, but the manifestation of conforming to the one basic force Tao. What accepts Tao is therefore virtuous in a cosmic sense. What opposes Tao is not – and cannot last, since opposing Tao is trying to counter the way the world works. Refusing to accept Tao is as futile as jumping up and down in an effort to escape gravity. It wears you down and gets you nowhere.

Using the word virtue for Te is not without risk, since it's already impregnated with meanings of European origin. It's from the Latin *virtus* and is mainly know to us from its ancient Roman and later its Christian use. There is also the concept of *virtù*, used for what used to be called manly virtues, including firmness and leadership skills.

Generally speaking, the European tradition regards virtue as moral behavior, the ability to live according to prevailing ideals. It's regarded as something calling for discipline and self-restraint, as if human beings otherwise slip into condemnable behavior. Those are virtuous who have the strength to resist their weaknesses.

Lao Tzu's Te is quite different in this respect. His virtue is one that occurs when we cease with our efforts. It's fol-

道

Te, virtue. Calligraphy by Stefan Stenudd.

lowing the natural way, wherefore we do it as soon as we let go of our ambitions – and only to the extent we are able to let go.

So, where the European tradition has it that virtue is what makes us rise above our natural impulses and instinctual cravings, Lao Tzu is clear about regarding virtue as something lesser than the natural state itself. To him, virtue is finding our way back to the behavior we were able before our conscious minds led us astray. Virtue leads us back to a life in harmony with Tao, the original Way.

The fundamental difference, then, between European and Taoist virtue is that the former regards man as a creature that should rise above nature and form a culture superior to it, while the latter teaches virtue as a method to return to nature.

So, to Lao Tzu virtue is only relevant for those who deviated from the Way. Those who live according to Tao are perfectly virtuous without having to consider it. Tao is ultimate virtue, simply because it is Tao, the Way it is and should be.

Especially when Lao Tzu writes "the greatest virtue," which he does frequently, he refers to living exactly according to Tao. Someone that virtuous is very relaxed in this, needing no effort whatsoever to remain on the Way.

Several of the Tao Te Ching chapters emphasize his argument for following the Way by showing what deviating from it leads to, inevitably: all kinds of misfortune and complications. That happens when virtue is abandoned or ignored, mostly because of misguided ambitions. So, whereas Tao is the ideal, Te is the manner by which to accomplish it.

That seems to be Lao Tzu's major distinction between the two terms, all through the book: He speaks about Tao

道

when describing the perfection hiding in the world, forming it and leading it right. When describing how mankind can get there, he talks about Te, the virtue we need to adopt. Te is the means by which we can live according to Tao.

The Sage

According to the Tao Te Ching, those are sage who understand the Way and act accordingly, which mostly means refraining from action. *Sheng Jen*, the Sage, is the ideal human being, who lives virtuously because he or she knowingly follows Tao. The Chinese expression doesn't specify gender.

Lao Tzu speaks repeatedly of the sages of ancient times. He shared this view on history with most if not all Chinese thinkers of antiquity. In their eyes, the time in which they lived was far inferior to the distant past in just about every way, especially regarding the virtue of society and its inhabitants.

This is far from a uniquely Chinese tradition. In most cultures all over the world, ancient times have been praised as superior to the present.

It was the same in our Western world for most of its history. The change came with The Enlightenment of the 18th century, although vaguely at first. They still praised what they called the noble savage of the past and of distant cultures hardly touched by European progress. Actually, the concept of a kind of ignorant bliss in the minds they called primitive is not that very far from Lao Tzu's ideal of humility, innocence, and a carefree attitude towards life.

A profound Western change of attitude towards the past evolved with the Industrial revolution in the 19th century. The advancement of technology and the progress of natural science soon rewrote history as one of development from a primitive state to one of increased refinement and advancement. Civilization was seen as a process of continuous improvement. Human wisdom was based on positivism, the idea that the methods of natural science are the only ones by which the world can be understood.

Still, praise of the distant past has remained for outstanding feats in certain exceptional periods of history, such as the philosophy of Ancient Greece and the art of the Renaissance.

To Lao Tzu, though, the view cherished by our modern world would be unfathomable. He was convinced that antiquity was better than his present in just about every conceivable way – certainly in regard to how the ancient ones lived according to the Way. The simple life he advocated would have no need for scientific and industrial development. Therefore, the future had nothing to add. According to Lao Tzu, the sage of the present would know to return to the ways of the sage of the past.

Tao Te Ching describes the personality and behavior of the Sage in several of its chapters, hoping for every reader to follow the noble example of such wisdom.

Non-action

Wu Wei, Non-action, is one of the most famous Taoist concepts, repeatedly pointed out in Tao Te Ching, the great Taoist classic. We should not hurry to act, since most things in the world take care of themselves if left alone. And when we act, we should do so cautiously, or we might destroy more than we solve.

Non-action is a central pillar of Taoist behavior and understanding. The world is run perfectly by Tao, the Way, so there is very little of human initiative needed. If we try to improve things, we are most likely to damage them and make the situation worse.

A Taoist waits before acting, and acts as little as possible when action is called for. Most problems go away by themselves. Lao Tzu repeats it many times, giving many different examples.

It's not so that he discourages action altogether. Sometimes we must act, but with regret and caution. Lao Tzu insists that the less we have to interfere with what happens around us, the better.

To him, the ideal society is the one that accepts what fate serves. He claims that in such case, fate is gentle.

Moderation

It can come as no surprise that the attitude preferred in a world run by Tao is one of moderation. Lao Tzu, the legendary author of the text, speaks with anger about those who are unable of it. He returns again and again to the importance of modesty and moderation in all things.

The word used in Tao Te Ching is *jian*, meaning frugality and restraint. Excess is straining on individuals and the whole society alike. Since nature ruled by Tao is a delicately tuned thing, there is no need for rocking the boat – neither by impulsive action nor by exaggeration.

True peace of mind can only be found in harmonizing with the Way, which is one of humility and stillness. People aiming elsewhere will only hurt themselves, without finding solace in the rewards they may think they get.

This ideal of moderation is shared by most philosophies

and religions the world over. Worldly possessions can't satisfy the human soul, nor can the things we normally connect to social success. Lao Tzu is consistent through his book about the illusive goals of ambition and the blessing of leaving it be.

That may be dull to many of us, but it is at the core of the philosophy of life presented in the Tao Te Ching.

Ruling

When the ideals are non-action and moderation, there's not much room for ruling in a Taoist manner. But Lao Tzu doesn't deny that rulers exist and are needed. He just presents firm restrictions as to their modus operandi.

A ruler should be hesitant and discreet enough to be all but invisible. A king ruling in accordance with Tao will do a lot of good – unnoticed, as if things took care of themselves. Well, according to Lao Tzu, mostly they do.

Although Lao Tzu is far from a ruler and just as far from wanting to be one, his text has plenty of chapters suggesting how one should act, or refrain from acting.

Legend has it that he was a civil servant in the royal court of Chou. But he left in disgust, riding a water buffalo. Just before crossing the border to unknown territories, he wrote the Tao Te ching upon the request of a border guard who was impressed by his wisdom.

It's evident in the text that he was familiar with the perspective of a ruler, and speaks quite frankly about it, sometimes so frankly that he would indeed need to leave the country afterwards.

道

War

The most extreme expression of ruling power is war. It's also what opposes the principle of Tao the most, Lao Tzu states quite clearly. War is nothing but utter failure to comply with the Way.

In several chapters, he points out just what a monstrosity war is and the sad state of things when it's unavoidable. It's not unfair to regard war, in the eyes of Lao Tzu, as the very opposite of a world guided completely by Tao.

Of course, it's a saddening final chord for the division into themes of Taoism to end with the condemnation of war and what induces it. The Tao Te Ching is not at all a text that ends in dismay, though not expressing that much trust in human transcendence. Its overall tone is light, not to say enlightening, in so much as it specifies what little is needed to make life on earth agreeable. Actually, the less is done, the more the world is likely to be pleasant.

The reason we end in thoughts about war is simply that it's the least significant of the seven themes extracted from the Tao Te Ching. Although I don't go so far as to number the themes in importance from one to seven, I dare say that they are arranged in an adequate order. As Lao Tzu says in chapter 38:

When the Way is lost there is virtue.
When virtue is lost there is benevolence.
When benevolence is lost there is righteousness.
When righteousness is lost there are rituals.
Rituals are the end of fidelity and honesty,
And the beginning of confusion.

He is most decisive in grading the qualities, finding flaws in all but Tao itself. Any book about Lao Tzu's Taoism should be arranged accordingly. So, the essence of Taoism is presented fairly only if it starts with Tao and then works its way downwards.

道

Ching, classic. Calligraphy by Stefan Stenudd.

Tao Quotes

Here are the 389 quotes extracted from the Tao Te ching, sorted by 51 topics (see the table of contents, page 5). Each quote has a reference to its chapter in the book.

The order of the topics follows more or less that of the basic themes, presented above, although expanding on them to include different angles of these Taoist principles.

The translation of the Tao Te ching quotes is as close as possible to the Chinese original, as we know it. That may make some of them rather cryptic – but then again, that's just as true for the Chinese text.

So, instead of changing the wording to something contemporary and easily accessible, I prefer leaving to the reader to make that transition. If one quote in itself makes little sense, it may be clarified by the other quotes on the same topic.

道

Tao, the Mysterious Way

The Way that can be walked is not the eternal Way.

[Chapter 1]

The Way is empty, yet inexhaustible, like an abyss!

[Chapter 4]

Obscure, like muddy waters.

[Chapter 15]

The Way is eternal. Until your last day, you are free from peril.

[Chapter 16]

I do not know its name. I call it the Way. For the lack of better words I call it great.

[Chapter 25]

The Way is ever nameless.

[Chapter 32]

The great Way is all-pervading. It reaches to the left and to the right. All things depend on it with their existence. Still it demands no obedience.

[Chapter 34]

It (Tao) is eternally without desire. So, it can be called small. All things return to it, although it does not make itself their ruler. So, it can be called great.

[Chapter 34]

Words spoken about the Way have no taste. When looked at, there's not enough to see. When listened to, there's not enough to hear. When used, it is never exhausted.

[Chapter 35]

道

Returning is the movement of the Way.

[Chapter 40]

The light of the Way seems dim.

[Chapter 41]

The progress of the Way seems retreating.

[Chapter 41]

The straightness of the Way seems curved.

[Chapter 41]

The Way is hidden and nameless. Still only the Way nourishes and completes.

[Chapter 41]

The whole world says that my Way is great like nothing else. It is great because it is like nothing else. If it were like everything else, it would long ago have become insignificant.

[Chapter 67]

Heaven's Way does not contend, yet it certainly triumphs. It does not speak, yet it certainly answers. It does not summon, yet things come by themselves. It seems to be at rest, yet it certainly has a plan.

[Chapter 73]

Heaven's net is very vast. It is sparsely meshed, yet nothing slips through.

[Chapter 73]

道

The Beginning

The nameless is the beginning of Heaven and Earth. The named is the mother of all things.

[Chapter 1]

From now back to antiquity, its (Tao's) name has not been lost. Thereby, see the origin of all.

[Chapter 21]

There was something that finished chaos, born before Heaven and Earth.

[Chapter 25]

All things in the world are born out of being. Being is born out of non-being.

[Chapter 40]

The world's beginning is its mother. To have found the mother is also to know the children. Although you know the children, cling to the mother. Until your last day you will not be harmed.

[Chapter 52]

道

Unity with Tao

Can you make your soul embrace the One and not lose it?

[Chapter 10]

Hold on to the ancient Way to master the present, and to learn the distant beginning.

[Chapter 14]

Knowledge of the eternal is all-embracing. To be all-embracing leads to righteousness, which is majestic.

[Chapter 16]

I alone am different from the others, because I am nourished by the great mother.

[Chapter 20]

The greatest virtue is to follow the Way utterly.

[Chapter 21]

The sage embraces the one, and is an example to the world.

[Chapter 22]

Hold on to the great image, and the whole world follows, follows unharmed, content and completely at peace.

[Chapter 35]

If I have just an ounce of sense, I follow the great Way, and fear only to stray from it.

[Chapter 53]

Profound virtue is indeed deep and wide. It leads all things back to the great order.

[Chapter 65]

道

When Tao Is Lost

When the great Tao is abandoned, benevolence and righteousness arise.

[Chapter 18]

Things exalted then decay. This is going against the Way. What goes against the Way meets an early end.

[Chapter 30]

The great Way is very straight, but people prefer to deviate.

[Chapter 53]

The Way of Nature

Heaven and Earth are not kind. They regard all things as offerings.

[Chapter 5]

Is not the space between Heaven and Earth like a bellows? It is empty, but lacks nothing. The more it moves, the more comes out of it.

[Chapter 5]

All things arise in unison. Thereby we see their return.

[Chapter 16]

All things flourish, and each returns to its source.

[Chapter 16]

道

Strong winds do not last all morning, hard rains do not last all day.

[Chapter 23]

If Heaven and Earth are unable to persist, how could man?

[Chapter 23]

Man is ruled by Earth. Earth is ruled by Heaven. Heaven is ruled by the Way. The Way is ruled by itself.

[Chapter 25]

What the Way is to the world, the stream is to the river and the sea.

[Chapter 32]

If Heaven were not clear it might rend. If Earth were not firm it might crumble.

[Chapter 39]

All things carry yin and embrace yang. They reach harmony by blending with the vital breath.

[Chapter 42]

Of all things, none does not revere the Way and honor virtue. Reverence of the Way and honoring virtue were not demanded of them, but it is in their nature.

[Chapter 51]

The river and the sea can be kings of a hundred valleys, because they lie below them.

[Chapter 66]

道 Tao

Leave the World Be

Conquering the world and changing it, I do not think it can succeed.

[Chapter 29]

The world is a sacred vessel that cannot be changed. He who changes it will destroy it. He who seizes it will lose it.

[Chapter 29]

Never take over the world to tamper with it. Those who want to tamper with it are not fit to take over the world.

[Chapter 48]

Malicious Knowledge

When wisdom and knowledge appear, great pretense arises.

[Chapter 18]

Those who understand others are clever, those who understand themselves are wise.

[Chapter 33]

The more clever and cunning people are, the stranger the events will be.

[Chapter 57]

People are difficult to rule, because of their knowledge.

[Chapter 65]

道

Tao

Know What You Don't Know

Not knowing of the eternal leads to unfortunate errors.

[Chapter 16]

Those who know it do not speak about it. Those who speak about it do not know it.

[Chapter 56]

Correct becomes defect. Good becomes ominous. People's delusions have certainly lasted long.

[Chapter 58]

Knowing that you do not know is the best. Not knowing that you do not know is an illness.

[Chapter 71]

Truly, only those who see illness as illness can avoid illness.

[Chapter 71]

The sage is not ill, because he sees illness as illness.

[Chapter 71]

True words seem false.

[Chapter 78]

True words are not pleasing. Pleasing words are not true.

[Chapter 81]

Those who are right do not argue. Those who argue are not right.

[Chapter 81]

Those who know are not learned. Those who are learned do not know.

[Chapter 81]

Enlightening Ignorance

Abandon wisdom, discard knowledge, and people will benefit a hundredfold.

[Chapter 19]

Abandon knowledge and your worries are over.

[Chapter 19]

I have the mind of a fool, understanding nothing.

[Chapter 20]

Those who seek knowledge, collect something every day. Those who seek the Way, let go of something every day.

[Chapter 48]

They Do Not Understand

My words are very easy to understand and very easy to practice. Still, no one in the world can understand or practice them.

[Chapter 70]

My words have an origin. My deeds have a sovereign. Truly, because people do not understand this, they do not understand me.

[Chapter 70]

That so few understand me is why I am treasured.

[Chapter 70]

道

Teacher and Student

A good person is the bad person's teacher. A bad person is the good person's task.

[Chapter 27]

The one who does not honor the teacher and the one who does not honor the task, although ever so knowledgeable, they are confused.

[Chapter 27]

The superior student listens to the Way and follows it closely. The average student listens to the Way and follows some and some not. The lesser student listens to the Way and laughs out loud. If there were no laughter it would not be the Way.

[Chapter 41]

Opposites Attract

When everyone in the world sees beauty, then ugly exists.

[Chapter 2]

What is and what is not create each other.

[Chapter 2]

High and low rest on each other.

[Chapter 2]

First and last follow each other.

[Chapter 2]

What's the difference between yes and no?

[Chapter 20]

道 **Tao**

What's the difference between beautiful and ugly?

[Chapter 20]

Heavy is the root of light.

[Chapter 26]

What should be shrunken must first be stretched.

[Chapter 36]

What should be weakened must first be strengthened.

[Chapter 36]

What should be abolished must first be cherished.

[Chapter 36]

What should be deprived must first be enriched.

[Chapter 36]

Misery is what happiness rests upon. Happiness is what misery lurks beneath.

[Chapter 58]

道

Paradoxes

The purest white seems stained.

[Chapter 41]

The grandest virtue seems deficient.

[Chapter 41]

The sturdiest virtue seems fragile.

[Chapter 41]

The most fundamental seems fickle.

[Chapter 41]

The perfect square lacks corners.

[Chapter 41]

The highest tone is hard to hear.

[Chapter 41]

The great image lacks shape.

[Chapter 41]

Sometimes gain comes from losing, and sometimes loss comes from gaining.

[Chapter 42]

What has no substance can penetrate what has no opening.

[Chapter 43]

The most complete seems lacking. Yet in use it is not exhausted.

[Chapter 45]

The most abundant seems empty. Yet in use it is not drained.

[Chapter 45]

道

The most straight seems curved.

[Chapter 45]

The most able seems clumsy.

[Chapter 45]

The most eloquent seems to stutter.

[Chapter 45]

Taste the tasteless.

[Chapter 63]

Make the small big and the few many.

[Chapter 63]

The Importance of Nothing

Thirty spokes are joined in the wheel's hub. The hole in the middle makes it useful.

[Chapter 11]

Mold clay into a bowl. The empty space makes it useful.

[Chapter 11]

Cut out doors and windows for the house. The holes make it useful.

[Chapter 11]

The value comes from what is there, but the use comes from what is not there.

[Chapter 11]

道

Tao

Non-Action

The sage acts by doing nothing.

[Chapter 2]

Can you comprehend everything in the four directions and still do nothing?

[Chapter 10]

Because he (the Sage) opposes no one, no one in the world can oppose him.

[Chapter 22]

The Way is ever without action, yet nothing is left undone.

[Chapter 37]

The highest virtue does nothing. Yet, nothing needs to be done. The lowest virtue does everything. Yet, much remains to be done.

[Chapter 38]

The value of teaching without words and accomplishing without action is understood by few in the world.

[Chapter 43]

The sage knows without traveling, perceives without looking, completes without acting.

[Chapter 47]

When nothing is done, nothing is left undone.

[Chapter 48]

Use justice to rule a country. Use surprise to wage war. Use non-action to govern the world.

[Chapter 57]

道

I do not act, and people become reformed by themselves.

[Chapter 57]

I am at peace, and people become fair by themselves.

[Chapter 57]

I do not interfere, and people become rich by themselves.

[Chapter 57]

Act without action.

[Chapter 63]

Those who act will fail. Those who seize will lose.

[Chapter 64]

He (the sage) wants all things to follow their own nature, but dares not act.

[Chapter 64]

The sage does not act and therefore does not fail, does not seize and therefore does not lose.

[Chapter 64]

道

Careful Action

Cautious, like crossing a river in the winter.

[Chapter 15]

Wary, as if surrounded by strangers.

[Chapter 15]

Although he travels all day, the sage never loses sight of his luggage carts.

[Chapter 26]

The best way to carve is not to split.

[Chapter 28]

Those who know when to halt are unharmed.

[Chapter 44]

Seal the openings, shut the doors, and until your last day you will not be exhausted. Widen the openings, interfere, and until your last day you will not be safe.

[Chapter 52]

The sage is sharp but does not cut, pointed but does not pierce, forthright but does not offend, bright but does not dazzle.

[Chapter 58]

Pursue without interfering.

[Chapter 63]

Lightly given promises must meet with little trust.

[Chapter 63]

Taking things lightly must lead to big difficulties.

[Chapter 63]

道

The sage regards things as difficult, and thereby avoids difficulty.

[Chapter 63]

People fail at the threshold of success. Be as cautious at the end as at the beginning. Then there will be no failure.

[Chapter 64]

Those who have the courage to dare will perish. Those who have the courage not to dare will live.

[Chapter 73]

The sage's Way is to act and not to contend.

[Chapter 81]

Prevention

Moderation means prevention. Prevention means achieving much virtue.

[Chapter 59]

Meet the difficult while it is easy.

[Chapter 63]

Meet the big while it is small.

[Chapter 63]

The most difficult in the world must be easy in its beginning.

[Chapter 63]

The biggest in the world is small in its beginning.

[Chapter 63]

道

The brittle is easy to shatter.

[Chapter 64]

The small is easy to scatter.

[Chapter 64]

What has not yet emerged is easy to prevent.

[Chapter 64]

Solve it before it happens. Order it before chaos emerges.

[Chapter 64]

A tree as wide as a man's embrace grows from a tiny shoot.

[Chapter 64]

A tower of nine stories starts with a pile of dirt.

[Chapter 64]

A climb of eight hundred feet starts where the foot stands.

[Chapter 64]

道

Patience

Who can wait in stillness while the mud settles?

[Chapter 15]

Who can rest until the moment of action?

[Chapter 15]

Moderation

Filling all the way to the brim is not as good as halting in time.

[Chapter 9]

Pounding an edge to sharpness will not make it last.

[Chapter 9]

(The five) colors blind the eye. (The five) tones deafen the ear. (The five) flavors dull the mouth.

[Chapter 12]

Racing through the field and hunting make the mind wild.

[Chapter 12]

道

He who holds on to the Way seeks no excess. Since he lacks excess, he can grow old in no need to be renewed.

[Chapter 15]

Those who stand on their toes are not steady.

[Chapter 24]

Those who take long steps cannot keep the pace.

[Chapter 24]

The sage avoids extremity, excess, and extravagance.

[Chapter 29]

Those who know when it is enough will not perish.

[Chapter 32]

Those who are content suffer no disgrace.

[Chapter 44]

To have enough of enough is always enough.

[Chapter 46]

Seal the openings, shut the doors, dull the sharpness, untie the knots, dim the light, become one with the dust. This is called the profound union.

[Chapter 56]

When leading people and serving Heaven, nothing exceeds moderation.

[Chapter 59]

The sage never strives for greatness, and can therefore accomplish greatness.

[Chapter 63]

By moderation one can be generous.

[Chapter 67]

道   Tao

Let the country be small, and the inhabitants few.

[Chapter 80]

Modesty

Because he (the Sage) demands no honor, he will never be dishonored.

[Chapter 2]

Not praising the deserving prevents envy.

[Chapter 3]

He (the Sage) does not show off, therefore he shines.

[Chapter 22]

He (the Sage) does not justify himself, therefore he is revered.

[Chapter 22]

道

Tao

He (the Sage) does not boast, therefore he is honored.

[Chapter 22]

He (the Sage) does not praise himself, therefore he remains.

[Chapter 22]

Those who show off do not shine.

[Chapter 24]

Those who are self-righteous are not prominent.

[Chapter 24]

Those who boast are not respected.

[Chapter 24]

Those who praise themselves do not prevail.

[Chapter 24]

The sage does not strive to be great. Thereby he can accomplish the great.

[Chapter 34]

Do not strive for the shine of jade, but clatter like stone.

[Chapter 39]

The sage wears coarse clothes, concealing jade.

[Chapter 70]

The sage knows himself, but does not parade. He cherishes himself, but does not praise himself.

[Chapter 72]

The sage acts without taking credit. He accomplishes without dwelling on it. He does not want to display his worth.

[Chapter 77]

道

Tao

Stay Where You Are

Those who stay where they are will endure.

[Chapter 33]

Without stepping out the door, you can know the world.

[Chapter 47]

Without looking through the window, you can see Heaven's Way.

[Chapter 47]

The longer you travel, the less you know.

[Chapter 47]

They can see their neighbors. Roosters and dogs can be heard from there. Still, they will age and die without visiting one another.

[Chapter 80]

Lowering Oneself in Humility

The sage puts himself last and becomes the first.

[Chapter 7]

Supreme good is like water. Water greatly benefits all things, without conflict. It flows through places that people loathe. Thereby it is close to the Way.

[Chapter 8]

Open, like a valley.

[Chapter 15]

Other people are joyous, like on the feast of the ox,
like on the way up to the terrace in the spring.
I alone am inert, giving no sign, like a newborn baby who has not learned to smile.

[Chapter 20]

道

I am wearied, as if I lacked a home to go to.

[Chapter 20]

Other people have more than they need, I alone seem wanting.

[Chapter 20]

Only I am clumsy, like drifting on the waves of the sea, without direction.

[Chapter 20]

Other people are occupied, I alone am unwilling, like the outcast.

[Chapter 20]

Knowing the bright, but clinging to the dark, you become a model to the world.

[Chapter 28]

Knowing honor, but clinging to disgrace, you become the valley of the world.

[Chapter 28]

The high must make the low its base.

[Chapter 39]

The highest virtue seems as low as a valley.

[Chapter 41]

If the sage wants to stand above people, he must speak to them from below. If he wants to lead people, he must follow them from behind.

[Chapter 66]

道   Tao

Benevolence and Compassion

The highest benevolence acts without purpose.

[Chapter 38]

The sage has no concern for himself, but makes the concerns of others his own.

[Chapter 49]

People turn their eyes and ears to him (the sage), and the sage cares for them like his own children.

[Chapter 49]

See others as yourself. See families as your family. See towns as your town. See countries as your country. See worlds as your world.

[Chapter 54]

Return animosity with virtue.

[Chapter 63]

I have three treasures that I cherish. The first is compassion. The second is moderation. The third is not claiming to be first in the world.

[Chapter 67]

By compassion one can be brave.

[Chapter 67]

The sage honors his part of the settlement, but does not exact his due from others.

[Chapter 79]

Heaven's Way is to benefit and not to harm.

[Chapter 81]

道

Tao

Desire

Free from desire you see the mystery. Full of desire you see the manifestations.

[Chapter 1]

Lessen selfishness and restrain desires.

[Chapter 19]

Without desire there is stillness, and the world settles by itself.

[Chapter 37]

There is no greater crime than desire.

[Chapter 46]

I have no desire to desire, and people become like the uncarved wood by themselves.

[Chapter 57]

The sage desires no desire, does not value rare treasures, learns without learning, recovers what people have left behind.

[Chapter 64]

道

Wealth and Greed

Not valuing wealth prevents theft.

[Chapter 3]

Keeping plenty of gold and jade in the palace makes no one able to defend it.

[Chapter 9]

Displaying riches and titles with pride brings about one's downfall.

[Chapter 9]

Searching for precious goods leads astray.

[Chapter 12]

Abandon cleverness, discard profit, and thieves and robbers will disappear.

[Chapter 19]

Those who know when they have enough are rich.

[Chapter 33]

Gain or loss, what is worse?

[Chapter 44]

Greed is costly. Assembled fortunes are lost.

[Chapter 44]

There is no greater misfortune than greed.

[Chapter 46]

When the palace is magnificent, the fields are filled with weeds, and the granaries are empty.

[Chapter 53]

Some have lavish garments, carry sharp swords, and feast on food and drink. They possess more than they can spend. This is called the vanity of robbers. It is certainly not the Way.

[Chapter 53]

道

People starve. The rulers consume too much with their taxes. That is why people starve.

[Chapter 75]

Heaven's Way is like stretching a bow. The high is lowered and the low is raised. Excess is reduced and deficiency is replenished. Heaven's Way reduces excess and replenishes deficiency. People's Way is not so. They reduce the deficient and supply the excessive.

[Chapter 77]

Who has excess and supplies the world? Only the one who follows the Way.

[Chapter 77]

The virtuous carry out the settlement, but those without virtue pursue their claims.

[Chapter 79]

The sage does not hoard. The more he does for others, the more he has. The more he thereby gives to others, the ever more he gets.

[Chapter 81]

道

Good and Bad

When everyone sees good, then bad exists.

[Chapter 2]

He (the sage) is good to those who are good. He is also good to those who are not good. That is the virtue of good.

[Chapter 49]

He (the Sage) is faithful to people who are faithful. He is also faithful to people who are not faithful. That is the virtue of faithfulness.

[Chapter 49]

The Way is the source of all things, good people's treasure and bad people's refuge.

[Chapter 62]

Fine words are traded. Noble deeds gain respect. But people who are not good, why abandon them?

[Chapter 62]

What Heaven detests, who knows why? Even the sage considers it difficult.

[Chapter 73]

Heaven's Way gives no favors. It always remains with good people.

[Chapter 79]

道 Tao

The Ancients

Ancient masters of excellence had a subtle essence, and a depth too profound to comprehend.

[Chapter 15]

The ancients said: Hulk to be whole.

[Chapter 22]

Why did the ancients praise the Way? Did they not say it was because you find what you seek and are saved from your wrongdoings?

[Chapter 62]

In ancient times, those who followed the Way did not try to give people knowledge thereof, but kept them ignorant.

[Chapter 65]

Nobility

Dignified, like a guest.

[Chapter 15]

The noble must make humility his root.

[Chapter 39]

Cultivate virtue in yourself, and it will be true.

[Chapter 54]

When much virtue is achieved, nothing is not overcome.

[Chapter 59]

道

Excellence

To retreat after a work well done is Heaven's Way.

[Chapter 9]

A good wanderer leaves no trace.

[Chapter 27]

A good speaker does not stutter.

[Chapter 27]

A good counter needs no calculator.

[Chapter 27]

A good door needs no lock, still it can't be opened.

[Chapter 27]

A good mooring needs no knot, still no one can untie it.

[Chapter 27]

道

Role Model

Being a model to the world, eternal virtue will never falter in you, and you return to the boundless.

[Chapter 28]

When the uncarved wood is split, its parts are put to use. When the sage is put to use, he becomes the head.

[Chapter 28]

Those who are unswerving have resolve.

[Chapter 33]

Inadequate Virtue

The highest virtue is not virtuous. Therefore it has virtue. The lowest virtue holds on to virtue. Therefore it has no virtue.

[Chapter 38]

道

Simplicity

The sage governs by emptying senses and filling bellies.

[Chapter 3]

The sage attends to the belly, and not to what he sees.

[Chapter 12]

Simple, like uncarved wood.

[Chapter 15]

Behave simply and hold on to purity.

[Chapter 19]

Being the valley of the world, eternal virtue will be full in you, and you return to the state of uncarved wood.

[Chapter 28]

Let people return to making knots on ropes, instead of writing.

[Chapter 80]

　　　　　道

Stillness

Attain utmost emptiness. Abide in steadfast stillness.

[Chapter 16]

Returning to the source is stillness. It is returning to one's fate. Returning to one's fate is eternal.

[Chapter 16]

Stillness is the ruler of haste.

[Chapter 26]

Stillness overcomes heat.

[Chapter 45]

Stillness is easy to maintain.

[Chapter 64]

Silence

A multitude of words is tiresome, unlike remaining centered.

[Chapter 5]

Those who are quiet value the words. When their task is completed, people will say: We did it ourselves.

[Chapter 17]

To be of few words is natural.

[Chapter 23]

Peace and quiet govern the world.

[Chapter 45]

道

Harmony

Where there is no conflict, there is no fault.

[Chapter 8]

Those who are one with deprivation are deprived of deprivation.

[Chapter 23]

The sage is one with the world, and lives in harmony with it.

[Chapter 49]

Harmony is called the eternal. Knowing the eternal is called clarity.

[Chapter 55]

Fear

Praise and disgrace cause fear.

[Chapter 13]

Praise leads to weakness. Getting it causes fear, losing it causes fear.

[Chapter 13]

The reason for great distress is the body. Without it, what distress could there be?

[Chapter 13]

Must one dread what others dread?

[Chapter 20]

If people are not afraid of dying, why threaten them with death?

[Chapter 74]

道

If people live in constant fear of death, and if breaking the law is punished by death, then who would dare?

[Chapter 74]

Rituals

When the Way is lost there is virtue. When virtue is lost there is benevolence. When benevolence is lost there is righteousness. When righteousness is lost there are rituals.

[Chapter 38]

Rituals are the end of fidelity and honesty, and the beginning of confusion.

[Chapter 38]

道

Tao

Unrest

When people are unsettled, loyal ministers arise.

[Chapter 18]

There is no greater disaster than discontent.

[Chapter 46]

Letting the mind control the vital breath is called force.

[Chapter 55]

You Get What You Give

Those who show no trust will not be trusted.

[Chapter 17]

Those who do not show trust will not be trusted.

[Chapter 23]

道

Tao

The Female

The valley spirit never dies. It is called the mystical female.

[Chapter 6]

Can you open and close the gate of Heaven and act like a woman?

[Chapter 10]

Knowing the manly, but clinging to the womanly, you become the valley of the world.

[Chapter 28]

A great country is like the lower outlet of a river. It is the world's meeting ground, the world's female.

[Chapter 61]

The female always surpasses the male with stillness. In her stillness she is yielding.

[Chapter 61]

道

Like a Child

Can you gather your vital breath and yet be tender like a newborn baby?

[Chapter 10]

Being the valley of the world, eternal virtue will never desert you, and you become like a little child anew.

[Chapter 28]

The one who is filled by virtue is like a newborn baby.

[Chapter 55]

Family

When family ties are disturbed, devoted children arise.

[Chapter 18]

Abandon benevolence, discard duty, and people will return to the family ties.

[Chapter 19]

Cultivate virtue in the family, and it will be overflowing.

[Chapter 54]

道

Yielding

Yielding, like ice about to melt.

[Chapter 15]

Hulk to be whole.

[Chapter 22]

Bend to be straight.

[Chapter 22]

Empty to be filled.

[Chapter 22]

Wear down to be renewed.

[Chapter 22]

Reduce to gain.

[Chapter 22]

The soft and weak overcome the hard and strong.

[Chapter 36]

Yielding is the manner of the Way.

[Chapter 40]

The softest in the world surpasses the hardest in the world.

[Chapter 43]

Holding on to the weak is called strength.

[Chapter 52]

Because he (the Sage) does not resist, none in the world resists him.

[Chapter 66]

道

The rigid tree will be felled.

[Chapter 76]

The rigid and big belong below. The soft and weak belong above.

[Chapter 76]

Nothing in the world is softer and weaker than water. Yet, to attack the hard and strong, nothing surpasses it.

[Chapter 78]

The weak overcomes the strong. The soft overcomes the hard. Everybody in the world knows this, still nobody makes use of it.

[Chapter 78]

Virtuous Ruling

Can you care for the people and rule the country and not be cunning?

[Chapter 10]

He who treasures his body as much as the world can care for the world.

[Chapter 13]

He who loves his body as much as the world can be entrusted with the world.

[Chapter 13]

In the world there are four greats, and the king is one of them.

[Chapter 25]

道

Good leaders reach solutions, and then stop. They do not dare to rely on force.

[Chapter 30]

If princes and kings could follow it (Tao), all things would by themselves abide, Heaven and Earth would unite and sweet dew would fall. People would by themselves find harmony, without being commanded.

[Chapter 32]

If princes and kings were not exalted they might be overthrown.

[Chapter 39]

What people loathe the most is to be orphaned, desolate, unworthy. But this is what princes and kings call themselves.

[Chapter 42]

Cultivate virtue in the town, and it will be lasting.

[Chapter 54]

Cultivate virtue in the country, and it will be abundant.

[Chapter 54]

Cultivate virtue in the world, and it will be universal.

[Chapter 54]

The one who rules like the mother lasts long.

[Chapter 59]

Ruling a great country is like cooking a small fish.

[Chapter 60]

道

When the world is ruled according to the Way, the ghosts lose their power. The ghosts do not really lose their power, but it is not used to harm people.

[Chapter 60]

When the emperor is crowned or the three dukes are appointed, rather than sending a gift of jade carried by four horses, remain still and offer the Way.

[Chapter 62]

When the sage stands above people, they are not oppressed. When he leads people, they are not obstructed. The world will exalt him and not grow tired of him.

[Chapter 66]

By not claiming to be first in the world one can rule.

[Chapter 67]

Excellent leaders of people lower themselves.

[Chapter 68]

To bear the country's disgrace is to rule the shrines of soil and grain. To bear the country's misfortunes is to be the king of the world.

[Chapter 78]

Rules for Rulers

The supreme rulers are hardly known by their subjects. The lesser are loved and praised. The even lesser are feared. The least are despised.

[Chapter 17]

In lightness the root is lost. In haste the ruler is lost.

[Chapter 26]

As soon as rules were made, names were given. There are already many names. One must know when it is enough.

[Chapter 32]

The more restrictions and prohibitions there are, the poorer the people will be.

[Chapter 57]

The more sharp weapons people have in a country, the bigger the disorder will be.

[Chapter 57]

The more laws and commands there are, the more thieves and robbers there will be.

[Chapter 57]

When the government is quite unobtrusive, people are indeed pure. When the government is quite prying, people are indeed conniving.

[Chapter 58]

If a great country yields to a small country, it will conquer the small country. If a small country yields to a great country, it will be conquered by the great country.

[Chapter 61]

道

A great country needs more people to serve it. A small country needs more people to serve. So, if both shall get what they need, the great country ought to yield.

[Chapter 61]

To rule by knowledge ravages the country.

[Chapter 65]

To be brave without compassion, generous without moderation, and rule without refraining from being first in the world, are certain deaths.

[Chapter 67]

When people do not dread authorities, then a greater dread descends.

[Chapter 72]

Do not make them (people) weary at their work. If you do not make them weary, they will not be weary of you.

[Chapter 72]

People are hard to govern. The rulers interfere with too much. That is why people are hard to govern.

[Chapter 75]

道

Longevity

Those who die without being forgotten get longevity.

[Chapter 33]

We go from birth to death. Three out of ten follow life. Three out of ten follow death. People who rush from birth to death are also three out of ten. Why is that so? Because they want to make too much of life.

[Chapter 50]

I have heard that the one who knows how to live can wander through the land without encountering the rhinoceros or the tiger. He passes the battlefield without being struck by weapons. In him, the rhinoceros finds no opening for its horn. The tiger finds no opening for its claws. The soldiers find no opening for their blades. Why is that so? Death has no place in him.

[Chapter 50]

Filling life exceedingly is called ominous.

[Chapter 55]

Things exalted then decay. This is going against the Way. What goes against the Way meets an early end.

[Chapter 55]

道

Life and Death

There is one appointed supreme executioner. Truly, trying to take the place of the supreme executioner is like trying to carve wood like a master carpenter. Of those who try to carve wood like a master carpenter, there are few who do not injure their hands.

[Chapter 74]

People take death lightly. They expect too much of life. That is why people take death lightly.

[Chapter 75]

Truly, only acting without thought of one's life is superior to valuing one's life.

[Chapter 75]

People are born soft and weak. They die hard and stiff.

[Chapter 76]

All things such as grass and trees are soft and supple in life. At their death they are withered and dry.

[Chapter 76]

The hard and stiff are death's companions. The soft and weak are life's companions.

[Chapter 76]

Let people take death seriously, and not travel far.

[Chapter 80]

道

Clarity

Seeing the small is called clarity.

[Chapter 52]

Use the light to return to clarity.

[Chapter 52]

Substance

Knowing the future is the flower of the Way, and the beginning of folly.

[Chapter 38]

The truly great ones rely on substance, and not on surface, hold on to the fruit, and not to the flower.

[Chapter 38]

Your name or your body, what is dearer? Your body or your wealth, what is worthier?

[Chapter 44]

道

Functionality

The separate parts make no carriage.

[Chapter 39]

The greatest vessel takes long to complete.

[Chapter 41]

Movement overcomes cold.

[Chapter 45]

What is well planted will not be uprooted.

[Chapter 54]

What is well held will not escape.

[Chapter 54]

War and Violence

Those who advice the ruler on the Way, do not want the world subdued with weapons.

[Chapter 30]

Thorn bushes grow where armies have camped.

[Chapter 30]

Battles are followed by years of famine.

[Chapter 30]

Weapons are ominous tools. They are abhorred by all creatures. Anyone who follows the Way shuns them.

[Chapter 31]

道

Weapons are ominous tools. They are not the noble ruler's tools. He only uses them when he can't avoid it.

[Chapter 31]

Peace and quiet are preferred. Victory should not be praised.

[Chapter 31]

Those who praise victory relish manslaughter. Those who relish manslaughter cannot reach their goals in the world.

[Chapter 31]

When many people are killed, they should be mourned and lamented. Those who are victorious in war should follow the rites of funerals.

[Chapter 31]

Those who defeat others are strong, those who defeat themselves are mighty.

[Chapter 33]

The fish cannot leave the deep waters. The state's weaponry should not be displayed.

[Chapter 36]

The forceful and violent will not die from natural causes.

[Chapter 42]

When the Way governs the world, the proud stallions drag dung carriages. When the Way is lost to the world, war horses are bred outside the city.

[Chapter 46]

Those who have compassion when they do battle will be victorious. Those who likewise defend themselves will be safe. Heaven will rescue and protect them with compassion.

[Chapter 67]

Excellent warriors are not violent.

[Chapter 68]

道

Excellent soldiers are not furious.

[Chapter 68]

Excellent conquerors do not engage.

[Chapter 68]

Warriors say: I dare not be like the host, but would rather be like the guest. I dare not advance an inch, but would rather retreat a foot.

[Chapter 69]

No misfortune is worse than underestimating the enemy. Underestimating the enemy, I risk losing my treasure.

[Chapter 69]

When equal armies battle, the grieving one will be victorious.

[Chapter 69]

The unyielding army will not win.

[Chapter 76]

When bitter enemies make peace, surely some
bitterness remains.

[Chapter 79]

Although there are weapons for tens and hun-
dreds of soldiers, they will not be used.

[Chapter 80]

Literature

There's a forest of books about Taoism, Lao Tzu, and the *Tao Te Ching*. It makes no sense to list them all, so I have chosen a few versions of the *Tao Te Ching* that I value or find significant in the continued exploration of Lao Tzu's thoughts. Less important works are also included, if they appeared before the present flood of Taoism texts emerged.

The subject is a hot one, so new books will appear as you read this, but I believe that some of the sources listed below will not that quickly be obsolete.

I have added a short comment to every version listed. It's just my personal opinion, so don't trust it any longer than you find it useful. Once you have started your own exploration of the subject, there's no guide more trustworthy than your own inkling.

As for the resources on the Internet, they change so quickly that I can only recommend a Google search (or whatever search engine is the most prominent one, when you read this). Notice that different spellings give partly different search results. For example, *Tao Te Ching*, *Dao De Jing*, and *Daodejing* searches differ, although the major search engines regard them as synonymous. The same is true for *Lao Tzu*, *Lao Zi*, and *Laozi*. Many complete translations of the *Tao Te Ching* are available on the Internet.

Tao Te Ching Versions

Ames, Roger T. & Hall, David L.: DAO DE JING
New York, Ballantine 2003.
A knowledgeable and rather daring version, which also presents the text in Chinese. The findings in Guodian are richly presented and included in the interpretation.

Blakney, Raymond B.: LAO TZU
USA, New American Library 1955.
A straightforward and clear version of the text, with elaborate comments and explanations.

Bynner, Witter: THE WAY OF LIFE ACCORDING TO
LAOTZU
New York, Day 1944.
An American version, which is also its subtitle. It's based on English versions of that time. In the effort to clarify the chapters, he allows himself to deviate quite far from Lao Tzu's text.

Chen, Ellen M.: THE TAO TE CHING
New York, Paragon 1989.
With a knowledge that is only surpassed by the categorical attitude, Chen presents a version that includes but is far from dominated by the Mawangdui manuscripts. Lots of facts are also included, as well as far-reaching personal interpretations of Taoist philosophy and how to apply it.

Cheng, Man-jan: LAO TZU: MY WORDS ARE VERY EASY
TO UNDERSTAND
California, North Atlantic Books 1981. Translated to English by
Tam C. Gibbs.
Cheng comments the chapters of the text in short lessons, focused on the principles of Taoism. The explanations are so short that they don't add much to the text itself. The Chinese text is included in the book.

Cleary, Thomas: THE ESSENTIAL TAO
San Francisco, Harper Collins 1993.

The East Asian Studies PhD has translated several Taoist and Buddhist texts, which have been published in a number of different volumes. This one contains the texts of both Lao Tzu and Chuang Tzu. His translation is competent, although his choice of words is sometimes odd, deviating from the usual solutions.

Crowley, Aleister: THE TAO TEH KING
1918. Several editions in print.
The famous occultist made his own very personal interpretation of the text, where the hexagrams of I Ching have also been used. Crowley is always worth reading, although it's not certain that he speaks according to the Tao of Lao Tzu.

Duyvendak, J.J.L.: TAO TE CHING
London, Murray 1954.
This professor in Chinese fills his version of the text with elaborate comments, including linguistic and philosophical aspects. This version is one of the few that met the approval of the prominent sinologist Bernhard Karlgren.

Feng, Gia-fu & English, Jane: LAO TSU: TAO TE CHING
London, Wildwood 1973.
This version is simple and rewarding, although it isn't always in accordance with prevalent opinion. It lacks commentaries, but is richly illustrated with both calligraphy of the chapters and mood-filled photographs.

Henricks, Robert: TE-TAO CHING
New York, Ballantine 1989.
The professor of religion manages a very trustworthy version of the text, based primarily on the manuscripts of Ma-

wangdui. Because of their order, he has reversed the words of the title. His comments are knowledgeable and precise. The Mawangdui texts in Chinese are also included. This is a major work on the Mawangdui findings.

Henricks, Robert: LAO TZU'S TAO TE CHING
New York, Columbia University Press 2000.
In this book, Henricks concentrates on the findings in Guodian, which are competently presented and examined. They are also compared to the Mawangdui and Wang Pi versions. The texts are included in Chinese. The problem with the book is that the order of the chapters is according to the findings, which makes it difficult to use as a reference. Hopefully, Henricks finds a solution for it in a coming edition.

Ivanhoe, Philip J.: THE DAODEJING OF LAOZI
Indianapolis, Hackett 2002.
The historian of Chinese thought has made a straightforward and clean translation of the text, a learned introduction to it, and comparisons between other translations. There are also many informative notes.

Jiyu, Ren: A TAOIST CLASSIC: THE BOOK OF LAO ZI
Beijing, Foreign Languages Press 1993.
This Chinese version translated to English also contains precise explanations that focus on how to understand the philosophy of the text and of Taoism. The interpretation and the perspectives are frequently quite far from those of most Western translators, which makes the book particularly interesting to study.

Julien, Stanislas: LE LIVRE DE LA VOIE ET DE LA VERTU
Paris 1842.
Julien was a professor in Chinese at the Paris University. His French version is the first printed one in a Western language. It is still in print, as a facsimile. Unfortunately, no English translation of it seems to be in print.

Karlgren, Bernhard: NOTES ON LAO-TSE
Bulletin of Östasiatiska Museet, nr. 47/1975. Offprint.
The world famous Swedish sinologist finally published, just three years before his demise, a version of the text. He did so in a way as modest as was his habit – in a magazine of the Stockholm East Asian Museum. His interpretation is precise and clarifying, but the comments are minimal. At the time of his interpretation, the findings in Mawangdui were not at his disposal.

Lau, D.C.: LAO TZU: TAO TE CHING
London, Penguin 1963.
This professor of Chinese literature gives a knowledgeable and clear interpretation of the text. The book also contains explicit comments and explanations. In later editions of this book, Lau includes the findings in Mawangdui and Guodian.

Legge, James: THE TAO TEH KING
London, Oxford 1891.
Legge's historically significant version has extensive explanations with many references to the Chinese pictograms and their meaning. Still, his translation is aged, especially because of its effort to create poetry, which makes it deviate considerably from the wording of the original.

Le Guin, Ursula K., and Seaton, J. P.: LAO TZU: TAO TE CHING
Boston, Shambhala 1997.
The famous fantasy and science fiction writer has made an elegant and very clear version of the text, in collaboration with a professor of Chinese. There are some comments, especially on how the chapters should be understood and on some linguistic aspects.

Mair, Victor H.: TAO TE CHING
New York, Bantam 1990.
This professor of Chinese bases his interpretation on the Mawangdui manuscripts. The books also contains extensive comments, especially those comparing the text with the ideas of ancient India.

Maurer, Herrymon: TAO: THE WAY OF THE WAYS
England, Wildwood 1986.
These interpretations and comments are aimed at explaining the text's spiritual content, which is done quite cryptically at times. In spite of the late date of this version, Maurer is unfamiliar with the Mawangdui manuscripts.

Mitchell, Stephen: TAO TE CHING: A NEW ENGLISH VERSION
USA, Harper & Row 1988.
This version, with very limited comments, seems to be made without noticeable knowledge of the Mawangdui manuscripts. Still, it has its merits as a simple and direct interpretation of the text. Later editions have made it to the bestseller lists.

Ryden, Edmund: LAOZI: DAODEJING
Oxford University Press 2008.
This version includes the Mawangdui and Guodian findings. The introduction and comments are learned, but the
wording in the translation sometimes gives the impression
of being dated. Ryden translates *Te* as "the life force," which
is similar to Arthur Waley's choice of "the power."

Star, Jonathan: TAO TE CHING
New York, Tarcher Penguin 2001.
The subtitle says that this is the definitive edition, which can
be discussed. But its material is very rich. The interpretation
of the text is given in Star's own words, but also word by
word parallel to the Chinese signs – completely according
to the Wang Pi version. There is also some other valuable
material in the book. It is quite useful to the devoted student
of the *Tao Te Ching*. In spite of its late publishing date, the
Guodian manuscript seems unknown to the author. That
might be corrected in later editions.

Ta-Kao, Chu: TAO TE CHING
London, Mandala 1959.
Ta-Kao allows himself to rearrange the text according to
what he feels is the most probable. That can be discussed.
Otherwise, his interpretation is straightforward and clear.
The comments are sparse.

Wagner, Rudolf G.: A CHINESE READING OF THE
DAODEJING
Albany, State University of New York Press 2003.
This is a translation of the Wang Pi commented version of
the *Tao Te Ching*, which is the most cherished one in Chinese

literature, a classic in its own right. The translation is very competently done, and so are the expert comments. The Chinese text is included. A must for the study of Wang Pi as well as Lao Tzu, but not an easy book to digest.

Waley, Arthur: THE WAY AND ITS POWER
London, Unwin 1934.
Waley's cherished version is assisted by elaborate comments and a long introduction. His interpretations of the chapters are not always the most probable, but his book has won the respect of several important sinologists.

Wilhelm, Richard: TAO TE CHING
London, Arkana 1985. Translated by H.G. Ostwald.
The first edition of Wilhelm's important interpretation in German was published in 1910. In later editions it was reworked considerably. The comments from 1925 are elaborate about both the language aspects and the ideas of the text. Wilhelm also made a widely spread version of the *I Ching*, where he had C. G. Jung write the foreword. It's a pity he didn't do the same with the *Tao Te Ching*.

Wing, R. L.: THE TAO OF POWER
New York, Doubleday 1986.
This version includes the Chinese writing, also calligraphy as well as other illustrations of interest. The writer has allowed himself the freedom of adapting some of the wordings to modern concepts. The findings in Mawangdui seem not to be used at all.

Yutang, Lin: THE WISDOM OF LAOTSE
New York, Random 1948.

The famous Chinese author made a pleasant interpretation, bordering on religious devotion. The book also contains a quantity of comments and explanations.